MW00768718

An Adventure in Northeast Tennessee
A Three-Day (Self-Guided) Tour

Faith Stahl

The Overmountain Press
JOHNSON CITY, TENNESSEE

ISBN 1-57072-023-1
Copyright © 1995 by Faith Stahl
All Rights Reserved
Printed in the United States of America

1 2 3 4 5 6 7 8 9 0

PREFACE

My husband and I are not native Tennesseans. Tennessee is our adopted state. My husband is a Pennsylvanian; I am a Virginian.

We came to East Tennessee from Pittsburgh, Pennsylvania, in 1946 (the year of Tennessee's sesquicentennial) and fell in love with the state and its people. We stayed.

In our native states, we were used to the hills and mountains. We felt at home surrounded by the Tennessee landscape. What was new to us was the rich Tennessee history and unique heritage that cannot be duplicated in any of the other forty-nine states. We were fascinated by the Watauga Association, the Battle of King's Mountain, the Lost State of Franklin, and Rocky Mount, the first capitol of the Territory South of the River Ohio. It all happened right here in East Tennessee, in overmountain country, as the pioneers spoke of it.

Both of us delved into Tennessee's rich history. When the Tipton-Haynes Historical Association was formed in 1965, we became charter members. My husband became the historian of the association. I became president and director of the Tipton-Haynes Historic Site in 1971, the year it opened.

When the bicentennial of the Lost State of Franklin came in 1984-1988, I was privileged to be the event's chairman. During the bicentennial, I organized the First Families of Franklin, which now numbers more than four thousand members. In 1993, these members formed the Lost State Historical Society, with every First Family member a lifetime member of the society.

When the opportunity came to participate in the coming Tennessee bicentennial of 1996, we thought that our fellow Tennesseans and our countrymen from other states ought to know this rich history and share with us the love affair we have had with our adopted state and, particularly, where it all began, East Tennessee. A self-guided tour of these important pre-Tennessee historical sites is a way of celebrating our state's history.

We hope this guide will enrich your knowledge of our beloved state and help you appreciate the heroism and sacrifice that not only made Tennessee a great state, but also the United States of America a great nation. Enjoy your stay in Tennessee. Linger long. Have a good time while you are with us.

—Faith Stahl

This tourbook is written to honor the memory of
Judge Samuel Cole Williams (1864-1947)
of Johnson City
Jurist, Tennessee Historian, and
Chairman of the Sesquicentennial in 1946

This tourbook is made possible because of the writings of Judge Samuel Cole Williams, and is in place for "Spotlight '95" and the bicentennial of Tennessee. Judge Williams was president of the "newly revived" Tennessee Historical Commission (1941), chairman of Tennessee's sesquicentennial in 1946, and, as a member of the Tennessee Historical Society, initiator of a movement that resulted in our prestatehood historic sites hosting visitors today. The Lost State Historical Society is dedicating "Spotlight '95" in his memory. Many of his major books are out of print, but they can be found in most Tennessee libraries.

ACKNOWLEDGMENTS

The Lost State Historical Commission is in charge of the "Spotlight '95" celebration honoring the memory of Judge Samuel Cole Williams, chairman of the Tennessee sesquicentennial in 1946 and, in retirement, prolific writer of prestatehood history. He is called "The Dean of Tennessee Historians."

This project would have been impossible without the interest in regional history shared by Archer and Judy Blevins of The Overmountain Press. Since publishing Pat Alderman's *The Overmountain Men* in 1970, they have published over one hundred regional and historical titles. Their list of prestatehood books is provided in Appendix J. Without their support and the help of Derik Shelor, editor, this guidebook would not have been written. The reprint of Samuel Cole Williams' *History of the Lost State of Franklin*, also by The Overmountain Press, is perfect for an in-depth reference to the events discussed in this guidebook.

The print of *The Battle of the Lost State of Franklin—Feb. 29, 1788* on the cover was sketched by John Alan Maxwell to illustrate Ray Stahl's 1970 story of the State of Franklin in *The Greeneville Sun*. Prints may be purchased at the Tipton-Haynes Historic Site.

For the Tennessee Homecoming in 1986, P. C. Snapp, of the Tennessee Planning Office of Upper East Tennessee, provided the Lost State of Franklin Historical Loop tour maps and a timeline chart. Michael White was the graphic artist. The timeline chart is being used here extensively. Refer to it often for help in understanding the twenty-seven years from wilderness to statehood.

Tom Hodge and the *Johnson City Press* have helped keep the interest in our project alive over the last ten years. Also, a "Before Tennessee" feature story contest by the Lost State Historical Commission is being promoted in Tennessee's newspapers for the year 1995.

My husband, Ray, has guided and critiqued my efforts. His paper about John Sevier, delivered to the Washington County Historical Society in 1994, is included and should be read before making this tour.

And to the many not named, I thank you for your encouragement.

—Faith Stahl

HOW TO USE THIS GUIDE

1. Obtain the latest brochures about each site, which will give the current hours of guided tours. These are available at hotels, visitors centers, and the various chambers of commerce.

2. Read the Foreword and become familiar with the timeline chart. Also read the short biography of John Sevier found on page 37.

3. The tours are designated *Day One, Day Two,* and *Day Three.* The guide always starts in Jonesborough, the oldest town in Tennessee. However, you may start at any point, go in any direction, and visit the sites in any order. The tours are coordinated with the timeline chart so that you can keep the chronology in mind.

4. As you drive each portion of the tours, the directions are on the left-hand page of this tourbook while brief descriptions of each stop are found on the right-hand page. The text of the historical markers seen on the tour are given in Appendix H.

5. At the end of each day, the tour stops at the last site visited.

TABLE OF CONTENTS

THREE PRESTATEHOOD GOVERNMENTS:
HISTORIC SITES IN THE FRANKLIN LOOP TOUR

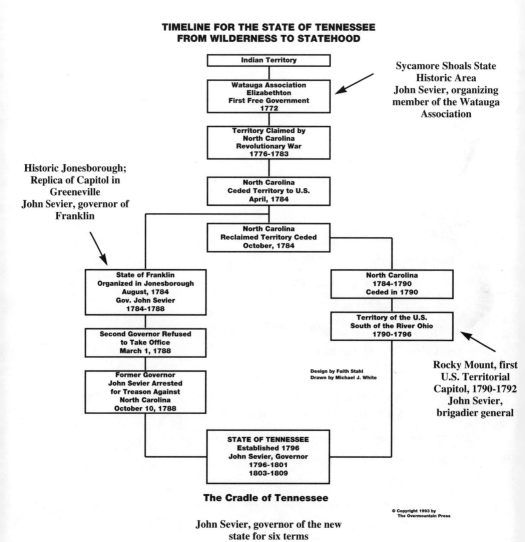

TIMELINE FOR THE STATE OF TENNESSEE
FROM WILDERNESS TO STATEHOOD

Indian Territory

Watauga Association
Elizabethton
First Free Government
1772

Sycamore Shoals State
Historic Area
John Sevier, organizing
member of the Watauga
Association

Territory Claimed by
North Carolina
Revolutionary War
1776-1783

Historic Jonesborough;
Replica of Capitol in
Greeneville
John Sevier, governor of
Franklin

North Carolina
Ceded Territory to U.S.
April, 1784

North Carolina
Reclaimed Territory Ceded
October, 1784

State of Franklin
Organized in Jonesborough
August, 1784
Gov. John Sevier
1784-1788

North Carolina
1784-1790
Ceded in 1790

Second Governor Refused
to Take Office
March 1, 1788

Territory of the U.S.
South of the River Ohio
1790-1796

Former Governor
John Sevier Arrested
for Treason Against
North Carolina
October 10, 1788

Design by Faith Stahl
Drawn by Michael J. White

Rocky Mount, first
U.S. Territorial
Capitol, 1790-1792
John Sevier,
brigadier general

STATE OF TENNESSEE
Established 1796
John Sevier, Governor
1796-1801
1803-1809

The Cradle of Tennessee

© Copyright 1993 by
The Overmountain Press

John Sevier, governor of the new
state for six terms

Training Ground for Leadership

FOREWORD

The approaching bicentennial of Tennessee, occurring in 1996, has to be understood against a background of events that covered twenty-seven years and occurred in the eastern section of the state.

Although the area comprising Tennessee was explored by white men as early as 1515 in the west and 1673 in the east, the first permanent settler did not build his cabin, plant his corn, and establish his home until 1769. Over the next twenty-seven years, the area we now know as East Tennessee was in near-anarchy and gave allegiance to five different governments before becoming a part of the sixteenth state, Tennessee.

After William Bean, in 1769, settled on Boones Creek, a tributary of the Watauga River, settlers poured into the mountains and valleys on the western side of the North Carolina mountains. So many came so quickly that, to prevent anarchy, it was necessary to establish a government. A group of law-and-order men organized the Watauga Association in 1772 and gave America its first written constitution. This government prevailed until the onset of the Revolutionary War.

Sensing that they could not survive against the opposition of both the British and the Indians, the citizens of the Watauga Association sought alliance, first with Virginia, and then with North Carolina. North Carolina received them in 1777. The union lasted until after the Treaty of Paris in 1783.

In April 1784, North Carolina ceded its western (overmountain) lands to the United States to pay its part of the war debts. The cession provided that within the next two years the United States was to form another state out of these lands. But the overmountain men did not wait for the national government to form a new state. They formed one themselves, calling it the State of Franklin in honor of American statesman Benjamin Franklin.

After the State of Franklin was formed, North Carolina, in October 1784, rescinded its offer and tried to take back its western lands. It took four years to wrest the government from the State of Franklin.

After the demise of the State of Franklin, the people of Watauga were once again under North Carolina sovereignty.

In 1790, the United States government (under President George Washington), having again been offered North Carolina's western lands, formed the Territory of the United States of America South of the River Ohio (also known as the Southwest Territory), which included the former lands of the State of Franklin. President Washington placed the political division under the authority of Governor William Blount and temporarily set the capitol at Rocky Mount (just north of present-day Johnson City). Washington charged the governor with preparing the territory for statehood.

In 1792, the capital of the Southwest Territory was moved to Knoxville, and four years later the population of the territory exceeded the census requirements for statehood. Governor Blount and his legislative council then organized the territory for statehood.

This bit of history has fascinated me and my wife, Faith, since we came to East Tennessee. It has caused us to delve into both Tennessee and pre-Tennessee history. We became involved with historical preservation sites such as Jonesborough, Tipton-Haynes farm, Rocky Mount, the State of Franklin capitol at Greeneville, and Sycamore Shoals.

Faith conceived the idea of a tour of these historic sites to help people visualize this complicated period of history in our state. Whether you are a Tennessean or visitor to our state before or after the bicentennial, we hope this tourbook will enhance your tour of and appreciation for the Volunteer State.

—Ray Stahl

Historic Jonesborough Visitors Center — 117 Boone Street
All three tours begin at this building.

DRIVING TOURS
A "Spotlight '95" Event
Introduction

The first two days will complete the "Lost State of Franklin Historical Loop" that was originally planned for one afternoon's driving during Tennessee Homecoming 1986. Two full days are allowed so that you can tour the sites plus have some bonus stops while near other points of interest. Day Three will include the Watauga Association and the Southwest Territory. This will complete a tour of all three prestatehood governments, truly an adventure in prestatehood history.

Day One

All tours are begun at the Jonesborough Visitors Center. Any extra time you have can always be spent browsing in the town's shops. The Heritage House in Erwin is a bonus. Be sure to check the museum's schedule as it is not open year-round. The marker about Gen. John Sevier's arrest is interesting for our tour only as a reminder of the incident. No one knows for sure where Widow Brown lived. Tipton-Haynes Historic Site is open year-round and has Boone's Cave, site of the Battle of the Lost State of Franklin, and a great tour story.

Day Two

Gov. John Sevier traveled the Nolichucky River Valley on one of his spirited horses while he was governor of Franklin and during his first three terms as governor of Tennessee. This area is on the National Register of Historic Places. The only State of Franklin building in Greeneville is the replica of the lost capitol building, so time is given to visit the Andrew Johnson Visitors Center. On the way back from Greeneville, you will visit the Davy Crockett Birthplace State Park. Crockett was born in the State of Franklin.

Day Three

The Sycamore Shoals Historic Area in Elizabethton is open year-round, but the Mansion, home of John and Landon Carter, is not. Bus tours are sometimes accommodated with prior planning. Rocky Mount, the U.S. Territorial Capitol from 1790 to 1792, is a living history site "where history lives today" and is a delightful place to end your adventure in prestatehood history.

The Franklin Loop

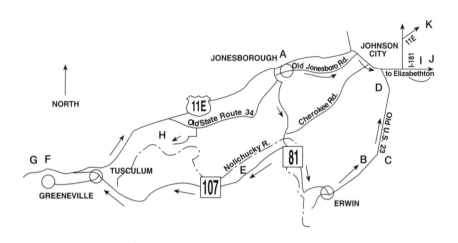

Drawn by Michael J. White—Local Planning Assistance Office, Dept. of Economic and Community Development

A Jonesborough — First Capital of State of Franklin
B Heritage House
C Widow Brown Plaque (1788)
D Tipton-Haynes Historic Site
E Plum Grove and Mt. Pleasant — Homesite of Governor John Sevier
F Replica of Lost State of Franklin Capitol (1785-1788)
G President Andrew Johnson Visitors Center
H David Crockett Birthplace (1786)
I Sycamore Shoals — Site of Fort Watauga
J Carter Mansion
K Rocky Mount

The Lost State of Franklin Territory

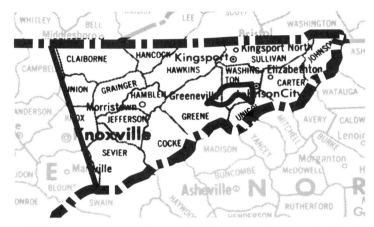

The East Tennessee counties outlined here were formerly the North Carolina counties of Washington, Sullivan, and Greene. They broke with North Carolina in 1784 to form the State of Franklin. Also shown is the Franklin Loop.

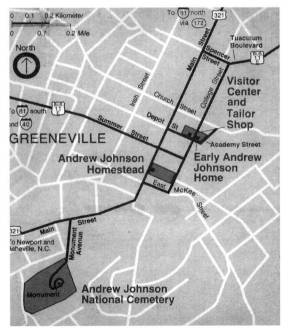

During the Day Two tour you will visit Greeneville, site of the Lost State of Franklin capitol replica and of the President Andrew Johnson Visitors Center.

DAY ONE / DIRECTIONS
Jonesborough to Johnson City via Erwin
—APPROXIMATELY 29 MILES—

Jonesborough
The Visitors Center and Museum in Jonesborough may be reached by turning south onto Boone Street at the Jonesborough traffic light on 11-E. Continue on Boone Street to the third large building on the right. The parking lot is south of this building. The center opens at 8:00 a.m. each day. Plan to spend several hours in Jonesborough during the three days.

Unicoi County Heritage Museum (Bonus Stop)
Leave Jonesborough Visitors Center parking lot, turning right onto Boone Street, and proceed 0.1 mile to Main Street. Turn right onto Main Street, and proceed 0.5 mile to join State Highway 81 South. Continue on 81 South for 8.2 miles, through the communities of Lamar and Embreeville, to the intersection of Highways 81 and 107. Join 107 (go straight ahead at the intersection) and drive 6.5 miles, crossing the Nolichucky River, to Erwin. In Erwin, go under the interstate to the first stoplight and turn left onto Erwin's Main Street (Hwy. 107). Follow this road for 2.2 miles. Unicoi County Heritage Museum is on the left. Enter on the left and go 0.1 mile, past the Erwin National Fish Hatchery, to the entrance of Heritage Museum.

Marker of John Sevier's Arrest for Treason
As you leave Heritage Museum, turn left onto 107. Follow this road for 1.5 miles. As you pass Dry Creek Road, you will cross a small bridge. Pull off to the right immediately after crossing the bridge. To the right is a stone marker telling of John Sevier's arrest for treason.

Tipton-Haynes Historic Site
After 1.6 more miles, the highway forks. Take the left fork and continue for 7.8 miles to the entrance to Tipton-Haynes Historic Site on the left. As you enter the site, there is an obelisk monument. Note the writing on this pillar as you enter the seventeen-acre site.

DAY ONE / SITE DESCRIPTIONS

Jonesborough

Within the Jonesborough Visitors Center is the Jonesborough-Washington County Museum (for which there is a small fee). A video presentation and several types of tours of Jonesborough are available. Jonesborough is Tennessee's oldest town and was the first capital of the Lost State of Franklin. The entire town is on the National Register of Historic Places.

Unicoi County Heritage Museum (Bonus Stop)

A large residence near the Erwin National Fish Hatchery, the museum houses in different rooms artifacts and memorabilia of the town's railroading, pottery making, Indians, etc., preserving the unique history of this small mountain town. (It is not open year-round.)

Marker of John Sevier's Arrest for Treason

On October 10, 1788, after the demise of the State of Franklin, Sevier was arrested at Widow Brown's home for what is called in history "The Spanish Intrigue." That same day, his son James was in New Orleans making arrangements for him to visit the Spanish there.

As the marker explains, John Sevier was not arrested for treason at this spot. In fact, historians have argued for three different locations, as Jacob Brown's widow and sons did not move here until after his accidental death. However, for the purpose of this guide that dispute is immaterial. This marker serves to introduce the story of the Spanish Intrigue, which is explained fully in Samuel Cole Williams' *History of the Lost State of Franklin.*

Tipton-Haynes Historic Site

The three-day skirmish called the "Battle of the Lost State of Franklin" was fought here in severe cold and a snowstorm on February 27, 28, and 29, 1788. March 1 was the date for the second governor to take office, but the attempt to form a new state ended here.

Col. John Tipton, who led the Washington District government for North Carolina, left three buildings which are still standing on the site: the double-crib horse barn, which housed his three race horses, Irish Grey, Don Quixote, and Diomed (named for the horse that won the first English Derby at Epson Downs in 1780), the double-crib granary, and the log house enclosed in the white frame house.

Trader James Needham wrote about the big spring and cave in 1673. The trees and plants behind the cave have been included in a nature trail for your enjoyment. (There is an admission fee.)

DAY TWO / DIRECTIONS
Jonesborough to Greeneville via Nolichucky Valley
to Davy Crockett State Park via 11E
—APPROXIMATELY 50 MILES—

Start at the Jonesborough Visitors Center and follow the same route as used on Day One for the first 8.8 miles to the junction with Highway 107.

Sevier's Mt. Pleasant and Plum Grove Homesite Area
Turn right onto 107 West and go 4.1 miles to Jackson Bridge Road. Turn right toward the river and park on the pull-off immediately on your right. Sevier owned a home (Mt. Pleasant) on the bluff to your right where only chimneys now stand. See the photograph on page 28. On the north side of the river he owned Plum Grove (exact site not identified).

Reproduction of Lost State of Franklin Capitol
Proceed 0.5 mile down Jackson Bridge Road, cross the bridge, turn around, and come back to 107. Turn right onto 107 and proceed 16.3 miles to the first stoplight, past Tusculum College. Turn left at the light onto 11E South and go 0.8 mile, then turn left onto Business 11E (Tusculum Boulevard). Continue for 2.6 miles, then, after passing Greeneville High School, turn left onto College Street. (There is no street sign for College Street.) Proceed for 0.2 mile to the log capitol and turn right into the parking lot. Note the sign on page 26.

President Andrew Johnson Visitors Center (Bonus Stop)
Turn right onto College Street and proceed 0.1 mile, through the first stoplight and to the next intersection. At this stop sign, turn left and enter the parking lot on your immediate left. The visitors center features self-paced tours on tape.

Davy Crockett Birthplace State Park
Retrace the route to the four-lane Highway 11E North, turning right toward Jonesborough, and continue on the four-lane for 9.5 miles. At the sign directing motorists to the state park, turn right and continue following the signs for 3.4 miles to the entrance.

DAY TWO / SITE DESCRIPTIONS

Sevier's Mt. Pleasant and Plum Grove Homesite Area

The site on the knoll (Mt. Pleasant) is owned by the federal government. Across the river was another home called Plum Grove. These sites are not developed, but this beautiful valley, first leased from the Indians by Jacob Brown, is the same valley John Sevier traveled.

After Sevier settled his family here around 1780, he lived in one or the other of the houses until 1803. He crossed this valley to Jonesborough and Greeneville while the State of Franklin existed, and during his first three terms as governor of Tennessee he traveled it to Knoxville. The last three terms he lived at Marble Springs, three miles south of Knoxville. Marble Springs is open as a historic site.

Reproduction of Lost State of Franklin Capitol

This replica was built to replace the building floated on rafts to Nashville for the centennial. The original was lost on the return voyage. A search into the mystery of the disappearance has proven unsuccessful so far. The building is unfurnished and opened only for special events.

President Andrew Johnson Visitors Center (Bonus Stop)

As a lad, Andrew Johnson was a tailor's apprentice. The owner had an employee hired to read history stories, usually to prevent boredom. After Johnson's marriage, his wife taught him to read and write. Johnson started his own tailor shop and continued the practice of having history read. He became active in politics and was elected vice president in 1860. He became president after Lincoln's assassination.

Davy Crockett Birthplace State Park

Davy Crockett was born in the Lost State of Franklin in 1786. He was restless and kept moving west in the state, as you can trace in the excellent museum exhibit. Before the TVA dams were built in the area for flood control, flash floods continually plagued the river valleys to the Mississippi River. Crockett lost several mills in floods.

Crockett was nominated for office as a joke, but he was a hit with the people north and south. They liked his picturesque appearance and speech. As a result he served three terms in the US legislature. When finally defeated, he went to Texas, where he was killed at the Alamo.

DAY THREE / DIRECTIONS
Part I
Jonesborough to Elizabethton via Johnson City
—APPROXIMATELY 19 MILES—

The first two days covered the Franklin Loop and included the Lost State of Franklin historic sites, along with some others. The last day starts with the government that came before the State of Franklin—The Watauga Association.

Sycamore Shoals Historic Area
Leave the Jonesborough Visitors Center, turning right toward Main Street. At Main Street, turn left heading toward Johnson City. Follow the winding road for 5.6 miles until it ends at the four-lane State of Franklin Road. Turn right and go 1.1 miles. Turn right onto University Parkway (Highway 321 South). Continue on 321 by East Tennessee State University and Pine Oaks Golf Course. Cross South Roan Street and go under the I-181 overpass and one railroad trestle. As you pass the trestle, take the off-ramp to Milligan Highway.

Turn right onto Milligan Highway and drive for 4.6 miles, through Happy Valley, veering left when the road forks. You will pass between Emmanuel School of Religion and Milligan College. (Robert and Alfred Taylor claimed Happy Valley as their home. The brothers ran against each other for governor of Tennessee in 1886. Bob won and served three terms. Alf Taylor served one term about twenty years later. It was Gov. Robert Taylor who planned the centennial celebration of Tennessee and had the log capitol of the State of Franklin floated to Nashville. He promised to bring it back and rebuild it, but the structure was lost on the return trip.)

At Milligan Highway's end, turn left onto the four-lane Highway 321. Continue straight on 321 for 2.1 miles; Sycamore Shoals Historic Area will be on your left.

The Mansion, Home of John and Landon Carter
As you leave Sycamore Shoals, turn left onto Highway 321. Turn left where 321 turns onto Broad Street, and follow 321 until it turns right. Do not turn but get in the middle lane and go straight through the intersection. After 0.2 mile, the Mansion will be on your left.

DAY THREE / SITE DESCRIPTIONS

Sycamore Shoals Historic Area

One point emphasized during the 1983 bicentennial of the signing of the Treaty of Paris was the fact that Fort Watauga (see the illustration on page 12) was the only fort west of the mountains that never gave up.

Fort Watauga was the anchor of the activity to the Mississippi River— a refuge for the settlers during enemy attacks. The same men who led the Watauga Association organized and led the State of Franklin and, later, the Southwest Territory and the State of Tennessee.

The fort was the scene of the Transylvania Purchase. The Cherokee Indians in 1775 met Judge Richard Henderson and sold him land claimed by themselves and other tribes. They also sold the land that the Wataugans had leased earlier, and Jacob Brown bought the Nolichucky Valley.

The Wataugans set up a land office, with Charles Robertson as clerk. (A descendant of Charles Robertson who recently received a "First Families of Franklin" certificate says that, contrary to what some historians have written, Charles and James Robertson were brothers. Charles had been in South Carolina because his wife was from there, but he later joined his brother here.)

Because Fort Watauga endured, the United States was able to nearly double its territory at the signing of the Treaty of Paris by claiming land extending to the Mississippi River.

The Mansion, Home of John and Landon Carter

John and Landon Carter's mansion is two stories. In colonial days, all two-story houses were called mansions. But the Carters were wealthy for their day, and the interior of the house shows it.

The glass windows were reportedly the first glass west of the mountains, and they were placed high in the walls. Extensive paneling, unusual mantels, and oil murals on the wood would certainly be impressive on the frontier. The Mansion was a good name for the house as it appeared in the wilderness two hundred years ago.

The Mansion is under the management of the same park service that manages the Sycamore Shoals Historic Area.

DAY THREE / DIRECTIONS
PART II

Elizabethton to Rocky Mount via I-181
—APPROXIMATELY 18 MILES—

The Watauga Association (visited in Part I) was the first independent government west of the Alleghenies. Now you are ready to visit the site of the government that started at Rocky Mount, after the State of Franklin.

Rocky Mount

Retrace your route on Highway 321. Continue on the four-lane Highway 321 to I-181. You will pass under one railroad trestle, then under the Milligan Highway overpass, and then under a second railroad trestle. Take the ramp going to I-181 North. Follow I-181 North for 3.5 miles to Exit 35A, which will put you on Highway 11E going toward Bristol. Follow 11E for 5.2 miles to the entrance of Rocky Mount on the right.

Fort Watauga at Sycamore Shoals was similar to this fort.
Engraving from G. R. McGee's *A History of Tennessee*.

DAY THREE / SITE DESCRIPTION

Rocky Mount

For two years, a private home (still standing at this site) served as the temporary capitol of the Territory of the United States South of the River Ohio. (It is easy to see why the title was shortened to Southwest Territory.)

William Blount was appointed by President George Washington to lead the preparation of the territory for statehood. He was considered the second handsomest man in the overmountain territory. (John Sevier is called the most handsome man by historians.) In the painting *Scene of the Signing of the Constitution of the United States* by Howard Chandler Christy (1940), the good-looking young man standing near the center of the picture is identified as William Blount.

William Cobb, a wealthy landowner and friend of Blount, allowed his home, Rocky Mount, to be used by the territorial governor as a temporary headquarters. In 1792, the territorial capital was changed to Knoxville.

Like Sevier, Blount had an aristocratic background; but both men were able to deal with the frontiersmen and gain their affection and respect. Also, they were both interested in obtaining land on the frontier.

Blount was a successful land speculator until he overextended himself, causing him to write a very uncharacteristic and indiscreet letter. This letter caused his impeachment trial by the U.S. Senate on January 10, 1799. His friends in Tennessee backed him loyally until his early death in 1800 at fifty-three years of age.

Descendants of the Cobb family have endowed this site, and it is the showplace of all our historic sites. You can spend one to five hours here and never be bored. (There is an admission fee.)

TIMELINE FOR THE STATE OF TENNESSEE
FROM WILDERNESS TO STATEHOOD

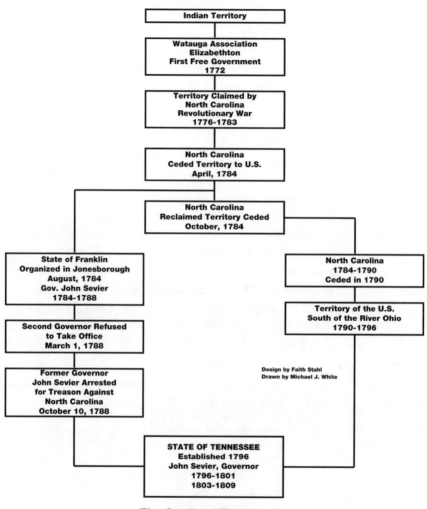

Indian Territory

Watauga Association
Elizabethton
First Free Government
1772

Territory Claimed by
North Carolina
Revolutionary War
1776-1783

North Carolina
Ceded Territory to U.S.
April, 1784

North Carolina
Reclaimed Territory Ceded
October, 1784

State of Franklin
Organized in Jonesborough
August, 1784
Gov. John Sevier
1784-1788

North Carolina
1784-1790
Ceded in 1790

Second Governor Refused
to Take Office
March 1, 1788

Territory of the U.S.
South of the River Ohio
1790-1796

Former Governor
John Sevier Arrested
for Treason Against
North Carolina
October 10, 1788

Design by Faith Stahl
Drawn by Michael J. White

STATE OF TENNESSEE
Established 1796
John Sevier, Governor
1796-1801
1803-1809

The Cradle of Tennessee

© Copyright 1993 by
The Overmountain Press

THE TWENTY-SEVEN YEARS
FROM WILDERNESS TO STATEHOOD

The Lost State of Franklin territory was located approximately just above
the position of the first "A" in "NORTH CAROLINA" on this map.
From McGee's *A History of Tennessee*.

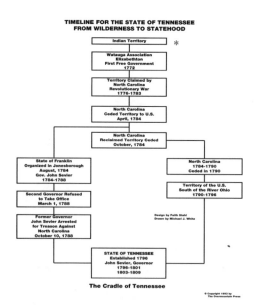

TIMELINE FOR THE STATE OF TENNESSEE
FROM WILDERNESS TO STATEHOOD

Indian Territory *

Watauga Association
Elizabethton
First Free Government
1772

Territory Claimed by
North Carolina
Revolutionary War
1776-1783

North Carolina
Ceded Territory to U.S.
April, 1784

North Carolina
Reclaimed Territory Ceded
October, 1784

State of Franklin
Organized in Jonesborough
August, 1784
Gov. John Sevier
1784-1788

North Carolina
1784-1790
Ceded in 1790

Second Governor Refused
to Take Office
March 1, 1788

Territory of the U.S.
South of the River Ohio
1790-1796

Former Governor
John Sevier Arrested
for Treason Against
North Carolina
October 10, 1788

Design by Faith Stahl
Drawn by Michael J. White

STATE OF TENNESSEE
Established 1796
John Sevier, Governor
1796-1801
1803-1809

The Cradle of Tennessee

© Copyright 1993 by
The Overmountain Press

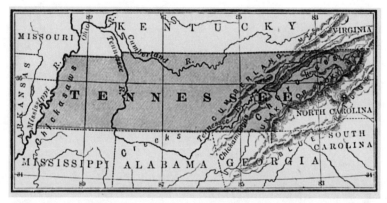

"When white people first settled on Tennessee soil, the Cherokee Indians lived in the mountains and valleys of what is now East Tennessee, and in the adjoining parts of North and South Carolina and Georgia…. The Chickamaugas lived…in the mountains about where Chattanooga now stands…. The Creeks lived along the Tennessee River, in what is now North Alabama…. The Chickasaws lived in North Mississippi and…in West Tennessee where, Memphis and Randolph now stand."

Central Tennessee was a vast hunting ground claimed by all these tribes, plus the Shawnees, of Indiana, and the Iroquois, of New York. No tribe dared live there.

"Deer, 'buffalo,' bears, 'elk,' swans, geese, ducks, and turkeys, and many other kinds of wild game were abundant."

The map and quotations are from *A History of Tennessee* by G. R. McGee, 1900.

- North Carolina's overmountain territory was sparsely settled by Indians two hundred years ago. *World Book Encyclopedia* lists about two hundred tribes in America, with a total population of less than one million. The Indians were friendly to the new settlers until the colonists started westward.
- The Indians had very little concept of ownership, and several tribes would claim the same land. All the Indian tribes listed on the map on the opposite page claimed the central section and met there to do battle.
- When Hernando de Soto came in contact with the Chickasaws in 1540, the tribe lived in villages of one-room log cabins. Ramsey's *The Annals of Tennessee* claims the Chickasaws had about five hundred warriors. The Cherokees in this period lived in wigwams.
- In 1769, the Cherokees attacked the Chickasaws and were defeated. As a result, they welcomed in 1772 the Wataugans' eight-year (some say ten-year) lease of Cherokee land in upper East Tennessee. Two years after signing the lease, the Cherokees sold the land of Middle Tennessee and Kentucky to Col. Richard Henderson in the Transylvania Purchase. At about the same time, the Wataugans bought their land and Jacob Brown bought the Nolichucky Valley.
- At this time, the Indians did not live in the Watauga area, but near the North Carolina line on the Little Pigeon River. They used the Watauga area for hunting and their Great Warrior Path, a major trail through the Cherokee Nation.
- The Cherokee, Chickamauga, and Creek Indians feared and respected John Sevier. Because of his expertise in resisting them, several settlements—including the overmountain fort of Watauga—survived when others failed.
- Around 1800, the Cherokees began building more permanent homes, owning slaves, and having tutors for their children. Sequoyah, a Cherokee of mixed blood, created a system of writing for his people.

TIMELINE FOR THE STATE OF TENNESSEE
FROM WILDERNESS TO STATEHOOD

Indian Territory *

Watauga Association
Elizabethton
First Free Government
1772

Territory Claimed by
North Carolina
Revolutionary War
1776-1783

North Carolina
Ceded Territory to U.S.
April, 1784

North Carolina
Reclaimed Territory Ceded
October, 1784

State of Franklin
Organized in Jonesborough
August, 1784
Gov. John Sevier
1784-1788

North Carolina
1784-1790
Ceded in 1790

Second Governor Refused
to Take Office
March 1, 1788

Territory of the U.S.
South of the River Ohio
1790-1796

Former Governor
John Sevier Arrested
for Treason Against
North Carolina
October 10, 1788

Design by Faith Stahl
Drawn by Michael J. White

STATE OF TENNESSEE
Established 1796
John Sevier, Governor
1796-1801
1803-1809

The Cradle of Tennessee

© Copyright 1983 by
The Overmountain Press

Elk and buffalo roamed Appalachia in the early days of America.
This engraving comes from *A History of Tennessee* by G. R. McGee

*Buffalo—The Engineers of the Wilderness

- Visitors are surprised when they hear about buffalo in East Tennessee. However, the pioneers followed the buffalo trails here two hundred years ago.
- The buffalo had to have salt twice a year, so entire herds would go to the nearest saltlick. The one nearest East Tennessee was northeast of Bristol, at Saltville, Virginia. Herds came from all directions.
- Buffalo always chose the easiest grade. They moved three abreast through the forest, making a five-foot-wide path. The ground was packed down like cement.
- In traveling to saltlicks all over Tennessee, the buffalo produced a network of trails, which was often used by the Indians and pioneers.
- *The Annals of Tennessee*, written in 1853 by Dr. J. G. M. Ramsey, the son of a pioneer, mentions several Tennessee saltlicks: French Lick, Mansco's Lick, Drake's Lick, and Bledsoe's Lick. He tells of numerous buffalo sightings:

  [Samuel] Calloway was at the side of [Daniel] Boone when, approaching the spurs of the Cumberland Mountain, and in view of the vast herds of buffalo grazing in the vallies between them, he exclaimed, 'I am richer than the man mentioned in scripture, who owned the cattle on a thousand hills—I own the wild beasts of more than a thousand vallies.'

- In Carter's Valley (near Rogersville), hunters in 1774 killed buffalo for meat within fifteen miles of the settlement. Fort Nashborough settlers would have starved without buffalo meat. The following is a description of French Lick near there:

  Where Nashville now stands they discovered the French Lick, and found around it immense numbers of buffalo and other wild game. The country was crowded with them. Their bellowings sounded from the hills and forest.

TIMELINE FOR THE STATE OF TENNESSEE
FROM WILDERNESS TO STATEHOOD

Indian Territory

Watauga Association
Elizabethton
First Free Government
1772   ✶

Territory Claimed by
North Carolina
Revolutionary War
1776-1783

North Carolina
Ceded Territory to U.S.
April, 1784

North Carolina
Reclaimed Territory Ceded
October, 1784

State of Franklin
Organized in Jonesborough
August, 1784
Gov. John Sevier
1784-1788

North Carolina
1784-1790
Ceded in 1790

Second Governor Refused
to Take Office
March 1, 1788

Territory of the U.S.
South of the River Ohio
1790-1796

Former Governor
John Sevier Arrested
for Treason Against
North Carolina
October 10, 1788

Design by Faith Stahl
Drawn by Michael J. White

STATE OF TENNESSEE
Established 1796
John Sevier, Governor
1796-1801
1803-1809

The Cradle of Tennessee

© Copyright 1993 by
The Overmountain Press

When John Sevier brought his whole family from the Valley of Virginia
(Shenandoah County) to help with the Watauga Association, packhorses had
to be used for much of the transportation. The illustration is from *A History
of Tennessee* by G. R. McGee, 1900.

- In 1763, at the end of the French and Indian War, the British government wanted to trade with the Cherokees and had promised them that all whites would be brought back across the mountains. This was enforced. That is the reason William Bean could be called the first *permanent* settler of Tennessee as late as 1769.
- At the Treaty of Fort Stanwix, negotiated by Virginia in 1768, the Indians sold the Crown the land between the Ohio and Tennessee rivers. A strong migration took place because the colonists assumed the tract was open for settlement.
- In 1769, William Bean located on the Watauga River (Boones Creek area); in 1770, James Robertson made the first trip to the area of present-day Elizabethton; in 1771, John Carter set up a store near Rogersville (Carter's Valley) and Jacob Brown settled on the Nolichucky River.
- A survey in 1772 showed they were south of the Virginia line on land claimed by North Carolina. Because they had leased the land from the Cherokees, the approximately seventy families refused North Carolina's order to leave.
- Using the town meeting pattern, in 1772 the settlers drew up a written "Articles of the Watauga Association" and appointed a Committee of Thirteen (legislative) and a Committee of Five (executive and judicial). John Sevier and James Robertson were members of the Committee of Five. In 1779, at the request of Judge Richard Henderson, Robertson took a group to Middle Tennessee (Fort Nashborough), leaving his friend John Sevier to carry on in East Tennessee.
- In 1775, two days after the Transylvania Purchase by Judge Henderson, the Wataugans bought their land.
- Too weak to fight both the British and their Indian allies in the impending revolution, the Watauga Association asked for the protection of North Carolina. The petition to be annexed to North Carolina was dated July 5, 1776, and signed by 113 men—only two had to use their mark.
- During the American Revolution, the settlers carried on with the same structural organization, but under the North Carolina government as the Washington District.

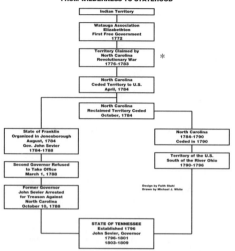

TIMELINE FOR THE STATE OF TENNESSEE
FROM WILDERNESS TO STATEHOOD

Indian Territory

Watauga Association
Elizabethton
First Free Government
1772

Territory Claimed by
North Carolina
Revolutionary War
1776-1783

North Carolina
Ceded Territory to U.S.
April, 1784

North Carolina
Reclaimed Territory Ceded
October, 1784

State of Franklin
Organized in Jonesborough
August, 1784
Gov. John Sevier
1784-1788

North Carolina
1784-1790
Ceded in 1790

Second Governor Refused
to Take Office
March 1, 1788

Territory of the U.S.
South of the River Ohio
1790-1796

Former Governor
John Sevier Arrested
for Treason Against
North Carolina
October 10, 1788

Design by Faith Stahl
Drawn by Michael J. White

STATE OF TENNESSEE
Established 1796
John Sevier, Governor
1796-1801
1803-1809

The Cradle of Tennessee

© Copyright 1993 by
The Overmountain Press

This monument is located in downtown Jonesborough, in front of the courthouse.

- By November 1777, the North Carolina Assembly had formed the Washington District into a county that included all of what is now Tennessee.

- North Carolina allowed each land holder, for a fee to be paid by 1779, to retain only 640 acres of the land that they had bought earlier. The North Carolina Assembly commissioned justices of the peace and sheriffs for the several courts formed. Jonesborough was named as the county seat.

- The settlers spent much of their time and energy protecting themselves from the Indians, who were encouraged by the British. A great many of John Sevier's thirty-five battles with the Indians occurred during this period.

- During the cold winter of 1779-1780, James Robertson sent several boats of immigrants the one thousand miles by water to Fort Nashborough, while he and some of the men from the immigrating families took the animals on the march over land. This opened up the Cumberland region.

- Ann Robertson Johnston, sister of James, was a young widow with three children of her own. She taught the party's children on the boat, which earned her the title of Tennessee's first female school teacher. Maj. John Cockrill, who commanded the soldiers guarding the flotilla, and Ann were married when they got to Fort Nashborough.

- Perhaps this small immigrant band did not know that Middle Tennessee was claimed by several tribes of Indians even though the Cherokees had sold it to Col. Richard Henderson. The cold winter and attacks by several tribes caused Dr. Ramsey, in *The Annals of Tennessee*, to call the voyage "…one of the greatest achievements in the settlement of the West."

- Back in the eastern settlement, Col. Patrick Ferguson, of the British Army, threatened to attack Fort Watauga, so John Sevier organized an army to attack him first. The Battle of King's Mountain, won by the western sharpshooters, was one of the decisive battles of the Revolutionary War. Colonel Ferguson was shot and killed as he tried to escape.

- After the Treaty of Paris in 1783, North Carolina ceded the overmountain territory to the federal government to pay the state's share of the federal debt. Once again the settlers had no government. (Congress had two years to accept the cession.)

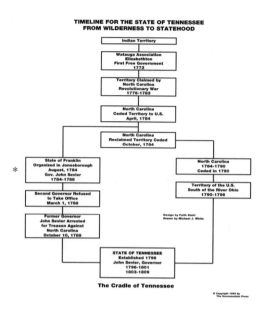

TIMELINE FOR THE STATE OF TENNESSEE
FROM WILDERNESS TO STATEHOOD

Indian Territory

Watauga Association
Elizabethton
First Free Government
1772

Territory Claimed by
North Carolina
Revolutionary War
1776-1783

North Carolina
Ceded Territory to U.S.
April, 1784

North Carolina
Reclaimed Territory Ceded
October, 1784

State of Franklin
Organized in Jonesborough
August, 1784
Gov. John Sevier
1784-1788

North Carolina
1784-1790
Ceded in 1790

Second Governor Refused
to Take Office
March 1, 1788

Territory of the U.S.
South of the River Ohio
1790-1796

Former Governor
John Sevier Arrested
for Treason Against
North Carolina
October 10, 1788

Design by Faith Stahl
Drawn by Michael J. White

STATE OF TENNESSEE
Established 1796
John Sevier, Governor
1796-1801
1803-1809

The Cradle of Tennessee

© Copyright 1993 by
The Overmountain Press

STATE of FRANKLIN

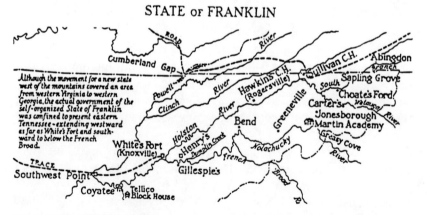

Although the movement for a new state
west of the mountains covered an area
from western Virginia to western
Georgia, the actual government of the
self-organized State of Franklin
was confined to present eastern
Tennessee - extending westward
as far as White's Fort and south-
ward to below the French
Broad.

The counties of Washington, Sullivan, and Greene (which reached to White's Fort, now Knoxville) of Western North Carolina were the only ones to break away to form the State of Franklin.

```
┌─────────────────────────────┐
│      State of Franklin       │
│  Organized in Jonesborough   │
│        August, 1784          │
│      Gov. John Sevier        │
│         1784-1788            │
└─────────────────────────────┘
```

* In 1782 Col. Arthur Campbell, of Virginia's Holston Valley, started the movement that eventually led to the State of Franklin.
* Campbell circulated a document to the settlers on the border of Virginia and North Carolina urging the organization of a group to request permission to form a state from land ceded by Virginia and North Carolina.
* The same men who had formed the Watauga Association led in forming a new government west of the Alleghenies.
* The families of the settlement were divided into captains' companies for taxing purposes and for the recruiting of militia to fight the Indians. Two men from every company were chosen—forty in all—to meet in Jonesborough on August 23, 1784, to form the new government.
* John Sevier was elected president, and John Carter's son Landon Carter, secretary. They formed an association to ask Congress to accept North Carolina's cession. They hoped eventually to form, with a contiguous part of Virginia, a new state.
* In October 1784, North Carolina rescinded its cession and appointed John Sevier to the high office of brigadier general of the militia of Washington District.
* At a meeting on December 14, 1784, in Jonesborough, a letter was read announcing that North Carolina had voted to reclaim the territory. Sevier spoke in favor of remaining faithful to the laws of North Carolina. Col. John Tipton and Rev. Samuel Houston spoke against it, reciting all the neglect of North Carolina. They were appointed to a committee to draw up a constitution. A meeting was set for November 1785 to vote on a constitution.
* At a meeting in March 1785, in Jonesborough, a new legislature was formed: John Sevier, governor; Landon Carter, speaker of the senate; Thomas Talbot, clerk; William Cage, speaker of the house of commons; and Thomas Chapman, clerk. David Campbell was elected judge of the superior court, and Joshua Gist and John Anderson, assistant judges.

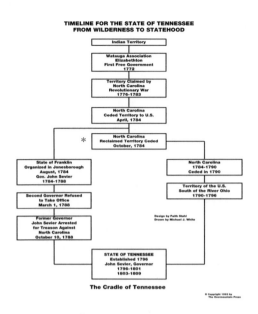

TIMELINE FOR THE STATE OF TENNESSEE
FROM WILDERNESS TO STATEHOOD

Indian Territory

Watauga Association
Elizabethton
First Free Government
1772

Territory Claimed by
North Carolina
Revolutionary War
1776-1783

North Carolina
Ceded Territory to U.S.
April, 1784

North Carolina
Reclaimed Territory Ceded
October, 1784

*

State of Franklin
Organized in Jonesborough
August, 1784
Gov. John Sevier
1784-1788

North Carolina
1784-1790
Ceded in 1790

Second Governor Refused
to Take Office
March 1, 1788

Territory of the U.S.
South of the River Ohio
1790-1796

Former Governor
John Sevier Arrested
for Treason Against
North Carolina
October 10, 1788

Design by Faith Stahl
Drawn by Michael J. White

STATE OF TENNESSEE
Established 1796
John Sevier, Governor
1796-1801
1803-1809

The Cradle of Tennessee

© Copyright 1993 by
The Overmountain Press

This historical marker is located on College Street in downtown
Greeneville, Tennessee, in front of the replica. It was placed there during
the Lost State of Franklin bicentennial.

> **North Carolina**
> **Reclaimed Territory Ceded**
> **October, 1784**

- In early 1784, before Washington County (overmountain country) was offered to the federal government, North Carolina had sold much of the choice land.
- After the remaining land was offered to pay North Carolina's war debt, land speculators persuaded the governor and the Assembly to rescind the offer. They argued that they could sell the land, pay their war debt, and have money left over.
- In October 1784, North Carolina reclaimed the land, but they were too late to stop the formation of the State of Franklin.
- During the 1785 constitutional convention in Greeneville, Tipton and Houston, who had been part of Colonel Campbell's Frankland movement in Virginia, led a movement for the state to be called State of Frankland (Anglo-Saxon for "Land of the Free") and to approve Reverend Houston's constitution. "After a hot debate and many tumultuous scenes," the report of the committee for Houston's constitution was rejected.
- A dissent was signed by nineteen delegates, and they left the convention. The names of the nineteen who signed a protest of the procedure are David Campbell, Samuel Houston, John Tipton, John Ward, Robert Love, William Cox, David Craig, James Montgomery, John Strain, Robert Allison, David Looney, John Blair, James White, Samuel Newell, John Gilliland, James Stuart, George Maxwell, Joseph Tipton, and Peter Parkinson.
- The convention accepted the constitution Sevier and his delegates supported. (For many years this constitution was lost. In 1904 it was found rolled up in a little paper box in the office of the Insurance Commission on the third floor of the capitol in Raleigh, North Carolina.)
- After the constitutional convention in Greeneville on November 14, 1785, as a result of the split in the advocates of Franklin, John Tipton became the leader of the "Antis," as Judge Williams calls them.
- John Tipton and his followers were chosen by North Carolina to run the rival government to Franklin. It took until 1788 to stop the followers of Sevier.

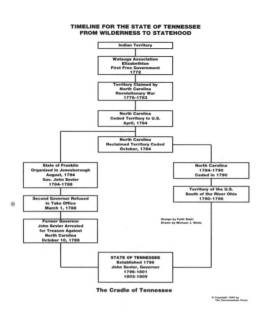

TIMELINE FOR THE STATE OF TENNESSEE
FROM WILDERNESS TO STATEHOOD

Indian Territory

Watauga Association
Elizabethton
First Free Government
1772

Territory Claimed by
North Carolina
Revolutionary War
1776-1783

North Carolina
Ceded Territory to U.S.
April, 1784

North Carolina
Reclaimed Territory Ceded
October, 1784

State of Franklin
Organized in Jonesborough
August, 1784
Gov. John Sevier
1784-1788

North Carolina
1784-1790
Ceded in 1790

Second Governor Refused
to Take Office
March 1, 1788

Territory of the U.S.
South of the River Ohio
1790-1796

Design by Faith Stahl
Drawn by Michael J. White

Former Governor
John Sevier Arrested
for Treason Against
North Carolina
October 10, 1788

STATE OF TENNESSEE
Established 1796
John Sevier, Governor
1796-1801
1803-1809

The Cradle of Tennessee

© Copyright 1993 by
The Overmountain Press

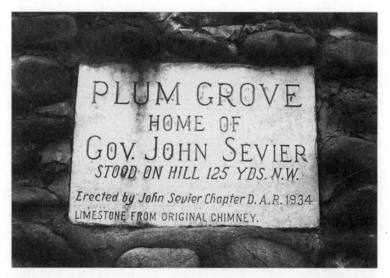

This plaque is located on the opposite side of Highway 107 from John
Sevier's Nolichucky homesite. John Sevier lived in two homes near this site
— one on the north side of the Nolichucky River, and one on the south.
Current research has called into question whether this is Plum Grove or
actually Mt. Pleasant.

| Second Governor Refused |
| to Take Office |
| March 1, 1788 |

- John Sevier lost none of his thirty-five battles with the Indians. He employed a technique later used by Napoleon: when outnumbered, attack. But he lost his skirmish against Tipton's supporters at Tipton's farm on February 27, 28, and 29, 1788.
- The winter of 1788 was bitterly cold. While Sevier was away fighting Indians, Tipton ordered his sheriff to bring Sevier's slaves and put them in the basement of his home with his own slaves. For their return, Sevier would have to pay the back taxes he owed North Carolina.
- Sevier brought 150 men, marched around the house with his drummer, and demanded the release of his slaves. Then he camped around the house and trained a cannon on the structure.
- Sevier's soldiers stayed near the campfires, rather than their posts, and about forty-five of Tipton's friends slipped into the house. When they got thirsty, two women under a flag of truce went to the spring. One was accidentally shot in the shoulder.
- A Tipton supporter went to Sullivan County to get help. On the morning of February 29, 1788, in a blinding snowstorm, help arrived and drove the forces of Sevier away.
- This "Battle of the Lost State of Franklin" was named by Mary Hardin McCown to differentiate it from "The Battle of Franklin," fought during the Civil War. As he lost this battle at the end of his term, the last three days of Sevier's governorship were the death knell of Franklin.
- The Franklin constitution called for the inauguration of a new governor on March 1, 1788. In 1787, Evan Shelby had been elected to succeed Sevier as governor of the State of Franklin. Shortly afterward, however, Shelby refused the position. No other governor was elected, so the State of Franklin ceased to exist.
- Sevier hated to give up and had some dialogue with the Spanish in New Orleans. This period, called "The Spanish Intrigue," led to his arrest for treason against North Carolina.

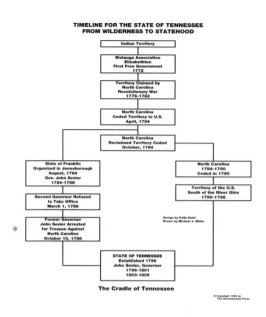

TIMELINE FOR THE STATE OF TENNESSEE
FROM WILDERNESS TO STATEHOOD

Indian Territory

Watauga Association
Elizabethton
First Free Government
1772

Territory Claimed by
North Carolina
Revolutionary War
1776-1783

North Carolina
Ceded Territory to U.S.
April, 1784

North Carolina
Reclaimed Territory Ceded
October, 1784

State of Franklin
Organized in Jonesborough
August, 1784
Gov. John Sevier
1784-1788

North Carolina
1784-1790
Ceded in 1790

Second Governor Refused
to Take Office
March 1, 1788

Territory of the U.S.
South of the River Ohio
1790-1796

Former Governor
John Sevier Arrested
for Treason Against
North Carolina
October 10, 1788

Design by Faith Stahl
Drawn by Michael J. White

STATE OF TENNESSEE
Established 1796
John Sevier, Governor
1796-1801
1803-1809

The Cradle of Tennessee

© Copyright 1993 by
The Overmountain Press

JOHN SEVIER HERO OF THE REVOLUTION
FIRST GOVERNOR OF TENNESSEE, WAS
ARRESTED AT THE HOME OF THE
WIDOW BROWN, ONE-HALF MILE NORTH-
WEST OF THIS SPOT, BY THE STATE OF
NORTH CAROLINA, IN 1788, FOR TREASON
BECAUSE OF HIS LOYALTY TO THE
STATE OF FRANKLIN.

ERECTED BY
UNAKA CHAPTER D.A.R.
1930

This plaque is located in the small park at the intersection of Highway
107 and Dry Creek Road, 1.5 miles north of Erwin's Heritage House.

Former Governor John Sevier Arrested for Treason Against North Carolina October 10, 1788

- France and Spain were allies of the colonists in the Revolutionary War, but this ended when France and Spain wanted the United States to remain east of the Allegheny Mountains.
- The United States, mainly because the settlements around Fort Watauga had survived against the Indians, extended its boundary to the Mississippi River at the Treaty of Paris in 1783.
- Spain, however, secretly strengthened its forces in New Orleans and, with the help of the Indians, planned to close the Mississippi River to navigation.
- Don Diego de Gardoqui came to New Orleans as *charge d'affairs*. Nashborough had just named its district Mero after the Spanish governor, and Gardoqui saw a chance to get Franklin to become an independent country and serve as a buffer to the United States.
- Sevier's son James was in New Orleans when John Sevier was arrested by North Carolina on October 10, 1788. On that very day, Gardoqui had given James a letter of introduction to Miro to arrange for John Sevier to visit New Orleans.
- That day, John Sevier was handcuffed at Widow Brown's in present-day Unicoi County and taken to Morgantown, North Carolina, for treason against North Carolina.
- Several stories are told of his being brought back to Tennessee by his friends before he could be tried.
- Sevier was elected the next year by Greene County voters as their representative in the North Carolina legislature.
- He was voted to be seated by the North Carolina legislature, appointed brigadier general of the Washington District, and elected to represent the district in Congress.
- Gen. John Sevier was the first representative sent to the U.S. Congress from west of the Allegheny Mountains.

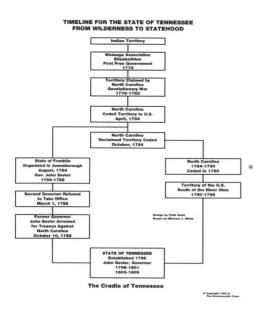

TIMELINE FOR THE STATE OF TENNESSEE
FROM WILDERNESS TO STATEHOOD

Indian Territory

Watauga Association
Elizabethton
First Free Government
1772

Territory Claimed by
North Carolina
Revolutionary War
1776-1783

North Carolina
Ceded Territory to U.S.
April, 1784

North Carolina
Reclaimed Territory Ceded
October, 1784

State of Franklin
Organized in Jonesborough
August, 1784
Gov. John Sevier
1784-1788

North Carolina
1784-1790
Ceded in 1790

Second Governor Refused
to Take Office
March 1, 1788

Territory of the U.S.
South of the River Ohio
1790-1796

Former Governor
John Sevier Arrested
for Treason Against
North Carolina
October 10, 1788

Design by Faith Stahl
Drawn by Michael J. White

STATE OF TENNESSEE
Established 1796
John Sevier, Governor
1796-1801
1803-1809

The Cradle of Tennessee

© Copyright 1993 by
The Overmountain Press

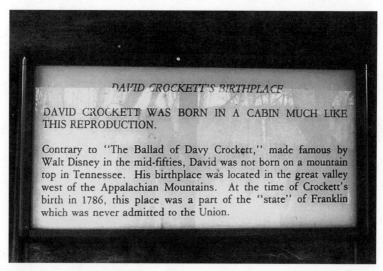

DAVID CROCKETT'S BIRTHPLACE

DAVID CROCKETT WAS BORN IN A CABIN MUCH LIKE
THIS REPRODUCTION.

Contrary to "The Ballad of Davy Crockett," made famous by
Walt Disney in the mid-fifties, David was not born on a mountain
top in Tennessee. His birthplace was located in the great valley
west of the Appalachian Mountains. At the time of Crockett's
birth in 1786, this place was a part of the "state" of Franklin
which was never admitted to the Union.

**David Crockett was born on August 17, 1786, a citizen of North Carolina
and of the State of Franklin.**

North Carolina
North Carolina **1784-1790** **Ceded in 1790**

- Both the State of Franklin and North Carolina's Washington County claimed sovereignty over the overmountain country, and both had functioning governments in the region by early 1786. Col. John Tipton was chosen senator of Washington County, and James Stuart and Richard White were chosen as members of the house of commons of the North Carolina legislature.
- A description of this period is given in Ramsey's *The Annals of Tennessee*:

> In the early part of the year 1786, was presented the strange spectacle of two empires exercised at one and the same time, over one and the same people. County courts were held in the same counties, under both governments; the militia were called out by officers appointed by both; laws were passed by both assemblies, and taxes laid by the authority of both states.... Every fresh provocation on the one side, was surpassed in way of retaliation by a still greater provocation on the other. The Judges commissioned by the State of Franklin held Supreme Courts twice in each year, in Jonesborough.... Tipton held courts under the authority of North-Carolina, at Buffalo, ten miles above Jonesborough....

- They raided each other's courts, stole papers and hid them, many of which were lost.
- Marriage licenses, deeds, and probate wills were issued by both states.
- Governor Sevier spent much of his time fighting against and negotiating a treaty with the Indians to protect the settlers who had moved south of the Holston and French Broad rivers.
- After Sevier's forces were defeated at the Battle of the Lost State of Franklin and no one filled his place as governor, Franklin ended on March 1, 1788.
- When North Carolina alone was again in charge of the territory they had shared with the State of Franklin, they refused to recognize the rights of settlers who had moved south of the Holston and French Broad rivers. For two years, until the western land was again ceded to the U.S. government and the Southwest Territory was formed in 1790, these settlers lived under an association for their own protection. Some call this the fourth independent government before statehood.

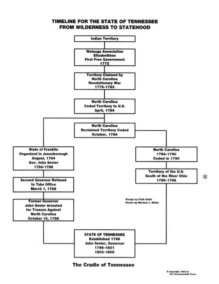

TIMELINE FOR THE STATE OF TENNESSEE
FROM WILDERNESS TO STATEHOOD

Indian Territory

Watauga Association
Elizabethton
First Free Government
1772

Territory Claimed by
North Carolina
Revolutionary War
1776-1783

North Carolina
Ceded Territory to U.S.
April, 1784

North Carolina
Reclaimed Territory Ceded
October, 1784

State of Franklin
Organized in Jonesborough
August, 1784
Gov. John Sevier
1784-1788

North Carolina
1784-1790
Ceded in 1790

Territory of the U.S.
South of the River Ohio
1790-1796   *

Second Governor Refused
to Take Office
March 1, 1788

Design by Faith Stahl
Drawn by Michael J. White

Former Governor
John Sevier Arrested
for Treason Against
North Carolina
October 10, 1788

STATE OF TENNESSEE
Established 1796
John Sevier, Governor
1796-1801
1803-1809

The Cradle of Tennessee

© Copyright 1993 by
The Overmountain Press

After Sevier was elected as Tennessee's first governor, the Tennessee legislature sent Blount to Congress as senator. He was the only senator ever impeached by the U.S. Senate. Blount had overextended himself by buying, it was reported, a million acres of land in Middle Tennessee. In trying to save the navigability of the Mississippi River, he had written a letter that fell into the hands of the president and the Senate. While Blount was momentarily absent from the floor, the letter (considered treasonous) was read to the whole Senate. After investigation, the U.S. Senate decided that they did not have jurisdiction and dismissed the case.

Blount's Tennessee friends stood by him and elected him to the Tennessee legislature, where he was made speaker of the Senate. They would have honored him further, but he died March 21, 1800, at age fifty-three.

Gen. Marcus J. Wright, in his *Life of William Blount*, says Blount was a patriotic man who was trying to help Tennesseans for whom "The United States was either unable or unwilling to secure the free navigation of the Mississippi River."

Territory of the U.S.
South of the River Ohio
1790-1796

- After the fall of Franklin, for two years, from 1788 to 1790, Col. John Tipton headed North Carolina's Washington District. The federal government organized the Territory of the United States of America South of the River Ohio (Southwest Territory) on May 26, 1790.
- On June 8, 1790, President George Washington appointed William Blount governor and Superintendent of Indian Affairs.
- Theodore Roosevelt says in *The Winning of the West*, Volume V, "Blount was a good-looking, well-bred man, with cultivated tastes; but he was also a man of force and energy, who knew well how to get on with the backwoodsmen, so that he soon became popular among them."
- President Washington appointees to help Blount were Daniel Smith, secretary of the territory; David Campbell, Joseph Anderson, and John McNairy, judges; John Sevier, brigadier general for Washington District; and James Robertson, brigadier general for Mero District.
- When Governor Blount first arrived, he made his residence with William Cobb, a wealthy farmer who lived near Washington Courthouse, between the Holston and the French Broad rivers.
- In 1793, Blount built what is said to be the first frame residence west of the Allegheny Mountains, at the corner of State Street and Hill Avenue, Knoxville. The rumor was that his wife would not join him until he built a home like she had in North Carolina. Blount Mansion in Knoxville is open as a historic site at the present time.
- In 1795, Governor Blount took a census and found there was a population of 77,262, of whom 66,650 were free inhabitants and 10,612 were slaves. A vote for statehood was taken, with 6,504 voting for and 2,562 voting against. An act for the admission of the state of Tennessee into the Union by the U.S. legislature was approved June 1, 1796.

JOHN SEVIER'S UNBROKEN FORTY-THREE-YEAR INVOLVEMENT IN THE STATE OF TENNESSEE

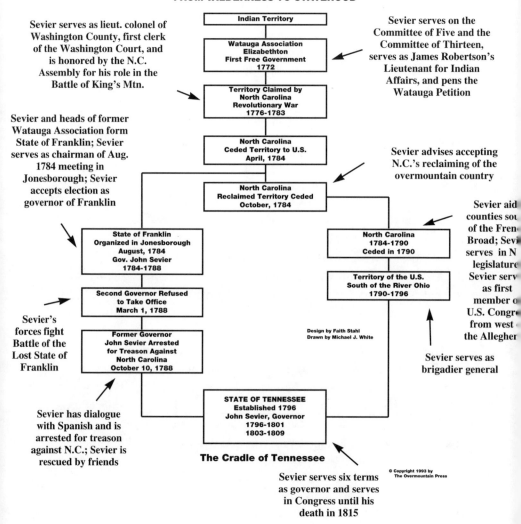

TIMELINE FOR THE STATE OF TENNESSEE
FROM WILDERNESS TO STATEHOOD

Sevier serves as lieut. colonel of Washington County, first clerk of the Washington Court, and is honored by the N.C. Assembly for his role in the Battle of King's Mtn.

Sevier serves on the Committee of Five and the Committee of Thirteen, serves as James Robertson's Lieutenant for Indian Affairs, and pens the Watauga Petition

Sevier and heads of former Watauga Association form State of Franklin; Sevier serves as chairman of Aug. 1784 meeting in Jonesborough; Sevier accepts election as governor of Franklin

Sevier advises accepting N.C.'s reclaiming of the overmountain country

Sevier aid counties sou of the Fren Broad; Sevi serves in N legislature Sevier serv as first member o U.S. Congre from west the Allegher

Sevier's forces fight Battle of the Lost State of Franklin

Sevier serves as brigadier general

Sevier has dialogue with Spanish and is arrested for treason against N.C.; Sevier is rescued by friends

Indian Territory

Watauga Association Elizabethton First Free Government 1772

Territory Claimed by North Carolina Revolutionary War 1776-1783

North Carolina Ceded Territory to U.S. April, 1784

North Carolina Reclaimed Territory Ceded October, 1784

State of Franklin Organized in Jonesborough August, 1784 Gov. John Sevier 1784-1788

Second Governor Refused to Take Office March 1, 1788

Former Governor John Sevier Arrested for Treason Against North Carolina October 10, 1788

North Carolina 1784-1790 Ceded in 1790

Territory of the U.S. South of the River Ohio 1790-1796

Design by Faith Stahl
Drawn by Michael J. White

STATE OF TENNESSEE Established 1796 John Sevier, Governor 1796-1801 1803-1809

The Cradle of Tennessee

Sevier serves six terms as governor and serves in Congress until his death in 1815

© Copyright 1993 by The Overmountain Press

General John Sevier, Father of East Tennessee
by Ray Stahl

Dr. Carl S. Driver, in his book *John Sevier, the Pioneer of the Old Southwest*, wrote, "Sevier was a pioneer and a leader of pioneers in a time which required perseverance and vision as well as sternness of character and singleness of purpose. He became Tennessee's first hero."

Samuel Cole Williams of Johnson City wrote, "Sevier was the idol of the people of his day.... Sevier has continued through succeeding generations to hold the first place in the hearts of the people of the Commonwealth."

Historian James R. Gilmore said of Sevier that he "was the founder and builder of that Commonwealth" and "the rear-guard of the Revolution, and the guardian and defender of the newly planted civilization beyond the Alleghanies."

Theodore Roosevelt placed Sevier with James Robertson, Daniel Boone, and others as prominent backwoods pioneers of the West and Southwest.

Sevier's forty-three years of public service, all spent in what we know today as East Tennessee, were phenomenal to say the least. If Ramsey can call James Robertson the "Father of Tennessee" and G. R. McGee can call him the "Father of Middle Tennessee," then surely John Sevier deserves to be called the "Father of East Tennessee."

On the marble shaft above his grave in Knoxville are inscribed these words:

> Pioneer, soldier, statesman and one of the founders of the Republic; governor of the State of Franklin; six times governor of Tennessee; four times elected to Congress; the typical pioneer who conquered the wilderness and fashioned the State; a projector and hero of King's Mountain; thirty-five battles, thirty-five victories; his Indian war-cry, 'Here they are! Come on, boys, come on!'

Who is this man, and where did he come from?

John Sevier's ancestry is both French and English. His paternal grandfather was a French Huguenot, who, according to Judge Samuel Cole Williams, "lived in the village of Xavier in the French Pyrenees." He and his brother fled to London following the Huguenot persecution after the Edict of Nantes was revoked by Louis XIV in 1685. The grandfather married a Miss Smith of London and became a prosperous merchant there. In France the family name was spelled "X-A-V-I-E-R," but the grandfather anglicized it when he came to England and renounced his French citizenship in protest of the persecution by the French.

Two of the grandfather's sons, Valentine and William, when they were quite young, ran away from home to America. They landed in Baltimore about 1740. Valentine, known in this country as Valentine Sr., moved into Augusta (now Rockingham) County in the Shenandoah Valley of Virginia. He became a member of Peter Scholl's military company in 1742. He married Joana Goode, of Woodstock, who bore him five boys and two girls. Valentine Sr. settled into business as a merchant, fur trader, and land speculator. He owned several tracts of land in the Shenandoah Valley and was known for his heavy gambling and drinking, traits which his son John never acquired.

EARLY LIFE IN VIRGINIA

John Sevier was born September 23, 1745, the oldest son of Valentine and Joana Sevier, in the Long Meadows district of Augusta County, Virginia, about six miles from the site of present-day New Market.

John had a good education for a boy of his day. He learned the basics from his mother. In 1753, his family moved to Fredericksburg, Virginia, when an Indian war broke out in the valley. In Fredericksburg, John took advantage of a good school for several years and worked in his father's store. When John was twelve years old, the family moved back to the Shenandoah Valley and he was sent to an advanced school in Staunton for four years.

In 1761, John Sevier left school at the age of sixteen and married Sarah Hawkins, fifteen, a member of a very respectable family in Hawkinstown in Shenandoah County, Virginia. He settled in Long Meadows and turned to farming and working in his father-in-law's store. In 1765, he bought from his father the family home and 378 acres of land, about forty miles south of Winchester and twenty miles north of Harrisonburg. It comprised the area of the present site of New Market, Virginia. John laid out the town of New Market, and the layout of the town today is much as he left it more than two centuries ago. Here he built a large warehouse and dwelling. He opened a store for selling dry goods, groceries, and furs for trading, and his father operated a tavern in the town. One of John's good deeds was the donating of three acres to the Baptists for a church, cemetery, and large courtyard. In 1770, he moved to Woodstock, the county seat of Shenandoah (or Dunmore) County.

Woodstock was also the residence of John Tipton, who was a justice of the peace, colonel in the militia, and vestryman for the Bedford Parish (the Anglican church in Woodstock).

According to Harry Long, the historian of Shenandoah County, "...Tipton and Sevier were well acquainted, while living in Shenandoah County, Virginia. John Tipton was present and served as justice on numerous occasions, where John Sevier appeared as plaintiff or defendant in suits brought before the Dunmore County Court. Not only was Tipton acquainted with Sevier's business and finances, but also his family's affairs and that of his in-laws." Mr. Long lists six times John Sevier appeared in Tipton's court as a defendant or plaintiff. He makes no comment on how well they got along in Virginia.

John Sevier was an Indian fighter for six years before he left Virginia. So impressed was Governor Lord Dunmore, the last of the royal governors of Virginia, that he commissioned him as a captain in the Virginia line— the same corps in which George Washington then held the rank of colonel.

COMES TO TENNESSEE

In 1771, John Sevier received an invitation from Capt. Evan Shelby to visit him at his cattle farm at King's Meadow (Bristol). He met James Robertson on this trip and learned of the fine work he was doing on the frontier. Sevier returned to King's Meadow again in 1772. On this visit he was present when the Watauga Association was formed.

When the Watauga Association was established, Sevier became a member of the Committee of Thirteen (the legislative body of the association) and the Committee of Five (the executive and judicial body). He also helped draft the constitution of the Watauga Association.

Sevier decided to return permanently after his 1772 visit, but before doing so sold all of his property in New Market and Woodstock. He took with him all of his family; his parents; his three brothers, Robert, Joseph, and Abraham, and their families; and his two sisters, Polly and Catherine, and their families and headed for Watauga Country. They arrived on Christmas Day, 1773, and established a home on the Holston. When Sevier was made an officer in the defense of Fort Caswell (Watauga), he took his family to live in the fort.

On July 5, 1776, Sevier was one of the representatives who asked for the Watauga Association to be brought under North Carolina's protection. The Wataugans feared that they would have insufficient strength to withstand the attacks of both the British and the Indians during the Revolutionary War.

In 1776, Sevier also became one of the first representatives of the provincial council of North Carolina and was elected lieutenant colonel of the Washington District. In the same year, he served in North Carolina's first constitutional convention.

In 1780, Colonel Ferguson of the British forces tauntingly threatened to devastate Western Carolina. With the help of Isaac Shelby, Sevier proposed meeting Ferguson head-on. Sevier, Shelby, and Col. William Campbell recruited seventeen hundred volunteers and met Ferguson at King's Mountain in South Carolina. The battle lasted but an hour. Ferguson lost his life, and 275 of his supporters with him, and 180 were wounded. American forces lost 30 lives and 60 men wounded. For his courage and bravery, the North Carolina legislature gave Sevier a vote of thanks, a sword, and a pistol.

In 1781, Sevier represented Watauga, of the Washington District, in the North Carolina legislature and was granted courts for his district by the legislature. At the same time, he was made a colonel in the militia and succeeded in organizing a militia of men between the ages of sixteen and fifty-six. When he returned home, he was elected clerk of the county and district judge.

After the Revolutionary War, the United States government asked states with western lands to cede these lands to the national government as a means of helping to pay the war debt. The idea was that as the U.S. government sold these lands, population would grow in these areas. When the census of each area reached sixty thousand, it would be eligible to apply for statehood.

In June 1784, the North Carolina legislature ceded its western lands to the United States with the understanding that within two years a state would be formed and that until then the territory would be under North Carolina sovereignty. The overmountain men claimed this to be an invitation to anarchy. The United States could do nothing for two years, and North Carolina wouldn't do anything. Consequently, they seceded from North Carolina and started making overtures of their own for statehood and an independent government. This caused North Carolina to rescind its cession offer and attempt to recover its western lands.

GOVERNOR OF FRANKLIN

Sevier was reluctant to form a separate government because it would interfere with his own land speculation, particularly in the Muscle Shoals section. He wanted to drop the whole issue. But the people were tired of North Carolina's do-nothing policy and were hungry for a new state. Almost against his will, the people persuaded John Sevier to accept their election of him as their governor. He accepted but later said that it was the biggest mistake he ever made.

A government was organized under the name of Franklin, a constitution was framed, and the mechanics of a government were set in order. However, within a short time Col. John Tipton led a campaign against Franklin and for loyalty to North Carolina. Two seats of government were established: one for Franklin, one for North Carolina. Sevier headed one, Tipton the other. People took sides. Confusion and turmoil occurred when the region had two sheriffs, two courts, taxes collected for two governments—two of everything. Altercations occurred between Tipton and Sevier on the streets of Jonesborough.

A crisis came when Tipton seized Sevier's slaves in payment of North Carolina taxes and Sevier, in an attempt to recover his slaves, challenged Tipton with a battle at Tipton's farm. The militia from Sullivan County came in a blinding snowstorm on February 29, 1788, and broke the three-day siege. This was the only battle John Sevier ever lost.

March 1, 1788, was the day a new governor was to take office, but the State of Franklin ended at this point. General Sevier had dialogue with the representatives of Spain, which caused his arrest for treason on October 10, 1788.

To make a short story, North Carolina regained its sovereignty over its western lands and Sevier eventually took the oath of allegiance to North Carolina.

Not long after Sevier took the oath of allegiance, he was elected to represent Greene County in the North Carolina Assembly. He was commissioned a brigadier general in the North Carolina militia, a commission he had refused when he was governor of Franklin. He was elected to the U.S. Congress from the Washington District of North Carolina, which at the time comprised what is now the whole state of Tennessee. He was the first person to serve in Congress from west of the Alleghenies. As a member of the North Carolina Assembly, he helped prepare North Carolina for statehood, and in the U.S. Congress he voted for North Carolina's admission into the Union.

In 1790, North Carolina again ceded its western lands to the U.S. government. As a member of Congress, Sevier voted for the federal government to accept the second cession of land by North Carolina. There was definite commitment this time to prepare the western lands for statehood, a challenge made by President Washington when he appointed William Blount governor of the Territory of the United States of America South of the River Ohio, often called the Southwest Territory. Rocky Mount, just north of Johnson City, was the capitol of the territory before it was moved to Knoxville. For six years Blount prepared the territory for statehood.

In the period of the Southwest Territory, Sevier served as a member of Blount's territorial legislature and served on a number of important committees. Blount applied for a commission for Sevier as brigadier general in the Washington District, which was conferred by President Washington.

Sixty thousand residents were required before a territory could apply for statehood. The Southwest Territory having a census of 77,262 on July 11, 1795, Blount applied for statehood and began framing a constitution and organizing the government.

FIRST GOVERNOR OF TENNESSEE

John Sevier was elected the first governor of Tennessee on February 6, 1796, with his inauguration March 30, 1796, and served six terms. He was inaugurated the first time in the Assembly Hall. His inauguration speech to the joint houses of the legislature was less than 150 words. Tennessee was admitted into the Union as the sixteenth state on June 1, 1796, by a vote of 43 to 30 in the House of Representatives.

After serving twelve years as governor, Sevier served three terms as Tennessee's congressman and was elected for a fourth term but died before learning of his win.

In the summer of 1815, President Madison had commissioned Sevier to settle the boundary line between Georgia and the Creeks. In executing the assignment, Sevier took sick and died September 24 of that year. He was buried in a cotton patch near Decatur, Alabama. In 1889 he was reburied in the courtyard at Knoxville, and a monument was erected to his honor.

I have not mentioned much about John Sevier's Indian fighting. It began in Virginia and continued in Tennessee for fifteen or more years.

One night Indians attacked Sevier's store in New Market, Virginia, and proceeded to rob him. He had only six men with him, but greatly outnumbered he routed the Indians and pursued them as they fled. He picked up their trail of dripping blood and traced them to their village.

He defeated them, scattering them in all directions, burned their village, destroyed their crops, and killed several of their warriors.

Sevier inaugurated a system of Indian warfare that called for an immediate frontal attack when outnumbered. He was often outnumbered twenty to one. This strategy of warfare was used by Napoleon years later.

Sevier used an Indian war whoop in his battles. A prisoner of war from King's Mountain said, "We could stand your fighting, but your cursed hallooing confused us; we thought the mountains had regiments instead of companies."

In more than twenty years of fighting with the Indians, Sevier was never wounded. He was careful for his men and always led them to victory, never losing one of his thirty-five battles. In all of his engagements, he lost only fifty-six men.

Why did Sevier leave Virginia? He had it made. He made money—a standard of success then as now. His friendship with Evan Shelby and James Robertson and his desire to become involved in early American government can be the only explanations.

Many have described John Sevier's unusual physical appearance, strong physique, and handsome bearing.

John Hillman, a Knoxville merchant who knew him personally, said of Sevier, "John Sevier was a very handsome man—probably the handsomest man in the state at that time. He had a noble bearing, real military, very conciliatory, without haughtiness. He knew how to get along with people better than any other I ever knew. He exhibited the best of his English and French Huguenot background."

This traditional story illustrates Sevier's unusual hold on the people, who often treated him as a demigod:

One time on his way from Knoxville to Virginia, word got out that Sevier would be passing through a rural community. He would be traveling by the church at about eleven o'clock. The church service was interrupted, and the whole congregation, including the minister, turned out to see him.

Sevier noted a small lad in the group and said to him, "Whom have we here?" and gave special attention to the boy. The boy turned to his father and said, "See, Pa, he is only a man."

Historian James Gilmore in *John Sevier as a Commonwealth Builder* (1887) made these statements about Sevier:

"No other man of equal talents and equal achievements has been so little noticed in American history."

"He was not of the ordinary type of backwoodsman. He was a gentleman born and bred; and in his veins flowed some of the best blood of the French and English nations."

"…he acquired as much of an education as was common to young gentlemen of the period—enough to enable him in after-years to be a ready and effective speaker and writer, and to associate on equal terms with the leading men of the country."

"I have conversed with a number of aged men who knew Sevier well in their boyhood, and they all agree in describing him as possessed of a personal magnetism that was nothing less than wonderful."

"Though [the Indians] recognized in him the Nemesis of their nation, they conceived for him a fanatical admiration, which at last deepened into a superstitious belief that he was the special representative of the INVISIBLE…this thought did more for Western civilization than a thousand Deckard rifles."

"I have called him a hero, a soldier, and a statesman; but he was more than all these: he was a civilizer, a great organizer, a nation builder. He found Tennessee a little cluster of log-houses, and he left it a great State, with happy homesteads, and smiling villages, and populous cities…and a population of nearly four hundred thousand souls."

"When the tidings of his death reached Tennessee, the whole State went into mourning. For the space of thirty days every public building was draped in black, and all State officials wore crape upon their arms."

John Sevier's Family

John Sevier was very fortunate to have had, over the years, two wives who were capable women and very supportive of his leadership on the frontier.

John Sevier was twenty-eight years old and Sarah Hawkins, his first wife, one year younger when they arrived in the Watauga territory at Christmas 1773. They had seven children, all under ten years of age. Sarah died in 1780 after their tenth child was born.

Joseph, born 1763, died 1824-January 1826
James, born 1764, died 1847
John, born 1766, died 1845
Elizabeth, born 1770, died 1790
Sarah, born 1770, died before 1839-1840
Mary Ann, born 1772, died 1853
Valentine, born 1773, died between 1839 and 1855
Richard, born 1775, died 1793
Rebecca, born 1777-1778, died 1799
Nancy, born 1780, died between 1825 and 1830

Later the same year, Sevier married a young woman, Catherine "Bonnie Kate" Sherrill. One of the favorite frontier stories is that earlier, when the settlers had all fled to Fort Watauga during an Indian attack, Sevier had saved her life. She was outside milking a cow when the attack began. An Indian chased her to the fort, and when Sevier helped her scale the wall, she fell "into his arms." Bonnie Kate bore him eight more children.

Catherine, born 1781, died 1827
George, born 1782, died 1849
Ruth, born 1783, died 1824
Joanna, born 1784, died 1823
Samuel, born 1785, died 1849
Polly, born 1786-1787, died 1850
Eliza, born 1790, died 1860
Robert, born about 1794, alive as of 1855

All of Sevier's eighteen children except one left descendants.

Appendix A

This guidebook is prepared as a companion work to be used with Judge Samuel Cole Williams' *History of the Lost State of Franklin*, first published in 1924. The 1933 revised edition was recently reprinted by The Overmountain Press.

The first eight chapters of Williams' book explain the background of the movement to organize the overmountain state.

Chapters II ("Genesis of the Franklin Movement") and VIII ("The Franklin Movement in Virginia") explain the part the Virginians played in the beginning. Col. John Tipton and Rev. Samuel Houston, both Virginians, presented a constitution to the Franklin convention in Greeneville in 1785. Chapter XIII ("The Second Constitutional Convention—1785") tells the details of Col. John Tipton and his followers' withdrawal from the new government.

To understand Governor Sevier's involvement in the Spanish Intrigue, read Chapter XXX, and for his arrest for treason read Chapter XXIX. Read also Chapter XVII ("Spain and Closure of the Mississippi—1786").

To understand the two years prior to the Southwest Territory (1788-1790) read Chapter XXVIII ("The Lesser Franklin").

Read Chapter XXXII ("The Second Cession and Afterwards") to understand Sevier's place in government until he was elected governor of Tennessee for six terms (the longest any governor has ever served).

Appendix B

In 1919 the Tennessee Historical Commission was organized to preserve the military records of soldiers who fought in World War I. By the 1930s the commission had become dormant. It was reorganized in 1941 by Governor Prentice Cooper, and with Judge Samuel Cole Williams as chairman the commission started in a new direction.

Judge Williams reorganized the commission statewide and directed the launching of the new *Tennessee Historical Quarterly*. He was a member of the board of the Tennessee Historical Society while chairman of the Tennessee Historical Commission. He took an active part in marking and preserving historical sites throughout the state.

In retirement, his goal in writing local history was to cover the important part of Tennessee's prestatehood history.

His first book, published in 1924, was *History of the Lost State of*

Franklin. He thought the State of Franklin was a significant manifestation of the spirit of separation which gave concern to national leaders. He reprinted all the available documents pertaining to the short lived state. Many are no longer preserved. A reprint of this book is available. See Appendix J.

His 1937 book, *Dawn of Tennessee Valley and Tennessee History*, was another of his major works. It covers the years 1515 to 1775, from de Soto's wandering through Tennessee to the beginning of the American Revolution. Its 492 pages cover the military, political, and diplomatic aspects of this period; the exploration of East Tennessee and the Cumberland Country; the influence of traders; the importance of Indians; and the schemes of the early land speculators.

On his eightieth birthday, Judge Williams finished a book designed to fill the gap between *Dawn of Tennessee Valley and Tennessee History* and *History of the Lost State of Franklin*. It was titled *Tennessee During the Revolutionary War.* It was published by the Tennessee Historical Commission in 1944, two years before the sesquicentennial. He died in 1947 before he could write about the Southwest Territory.

Although many of his books are out of print, they are available in most Tennessee libraries. Also, the first volume of John Trotwood Moore's *Tennessee: the Volunteer State, 1769-1923* and Theodore Roosevelt's multi-volume work, *The Winning of the West*, are good source materials.

Appendix C

A copy of the constitution of the State of Franklin is in Appendix A of *History of the Lost State of Franklin* by Williams. This was the constitution preferred by Governor Sevier in Greeneville.

The constitution was lost for years until a copy was found in the early 1900s in an office in Raleigh. John Trotwood Moore copied it in 1923 and Judge Williams in 1924 in his *History of the Lost State of Franklin*.

Appendix D

A petition written in 1787 to North Carolina by inhabitants of the western country is in Appendix B of the Williams book. Literally hundreds of signatures were on it.

Appendix E

Appendix C of the Williams book provides the proceedings of a convention in 1789 during the period of waiting for the Southwest Territory to be formed. It shows some of the problems the settlers faced.

Appendix F

The newly organized Lost State Historical Society (1993) is composed of more than 4,000 life members, all of whom hold "First Families of Franklin" certificates. The society is governed by the ten-member Lost State Historical Commission.

The Lost State Historical Commission
(The Executive Board—Non-members Eligible)

Archer M. Blevins, Publisher, The Overmountain Press

Betsey Bowman, Member of the board of proposed Lost State outdoor drama, Tusculum College

Dr. Evelyn Ells Elmer, Treasurer, Retired University Professor

James Epps III, Attorney, Member Tennessee Bicentennial Commission

Cherel Henderson, Assistant to Director, East Tennessee Historical Society

Tom Hodge, Editorial Director, *Johnson City Press*, Washington County Bicentennial Commission

Rhonda Lane, Secretary of the Executive Board

Faith Stahl, Chairman, Originator of First Families of Franklin, Book of Records and Certificate of Membership, 1984, Organizer of The Lost State Historical Society, August 1993

Ray Stahl, Historian, City Historian of Johnson City

J. D. Swartz, Former owner of Aquone—Home of Judge Samuel Cole Williams, who preserved the story of the lost state in his book *History of the Lost State of Franklin*, 1924. In October 1993, Mr. Swartz secured for the home the designation of being listed on the National Register of Historic Places.

Appendix G

Below are listed the names of leading pioneers who participated in and against the Franklin movement. A short biography of each is given in Samuel Cole Williams' *History of the Lost State of Franklin* and can be found on the bracketed page number.

The Franklinites

John Anderson [315]
William Cage [313]
Arthur Campbell [291]
David Campbell [316]
Judge David Campbell [298]
Landon Carter [299]
Gilbert Christian [303]
William Cocke [294]
Henry Conway [310]
Samuel Doak [317]
George Doherty [317]
Stockley Donelson [313]
Augustus Christian George Elholm [309]
Nathaniel Evans [319]
Joshua Gist [314]
Samuel Handley [319]
Joseph Hardin [304]
Samuel Houston [320]
Daniel Kennedy [307]
David Looney [322]
Moses Looney [322]
John Menefee [315]
William Murphey [323]
Samuel Newell [323]

Alexander Outlaw [324]
Francis A. Ramsey [311]
James Reese [325]
Charles Robertson [306]
Charles Robertson (or Robinson) [325]
James Roddy [326]
John Sevier [289]
Valentine Sevier II [326]
Andrew Taylor [327]
Peter Turney [327]
George Vincent [328]
Samuel Wear (or Weir) [328]
James White [301]

The Antis

Thomas Hutchings [335]
Robert Love [336]
Thomas Love [336]
Joseph Martin [331]
George Maxwell [337]
Peter Parkinson [337]
Evan Shelby [330]
James Stuart [337]
John Tipton [334]

Appendix H
Tennessee Historical Markers on Driving Tour
Quoted from *Tennessee Historical Markers*
Published by the Tennessee Historical Commission
DAY ONE
(Tenn. 81) *Washington County, 4.5 miles south of Jonesboro*
1 A 59—Cherokee Church—Holston Baptist Association
This Baptist church was organized the first Sunday in September, 1783. Here, the fourth Saturday in October, 1786, Holston Association was organized with Tidence Lane moderator and Wm. Murphy clerk. Seven churches were represented. This was the first Baptist Association in Tennessee.

(Tenn. 81) *Washington County, 4.5 miles south of Jonesboro*
1 A 79—Old Dutch Meeting House
1¼ mile is the site of the Immanuel Lutheran Church and cemetery. Organized about 1807; reported in 1811 to the North Carolina Synod, and became charter member of Tennessee Synod in 1820. In its early years, services were held in both German and English. The church was disbanded about 1870.

(Tenn. 81) *Washington County, south of Lamar School*
1 A 25—Jacob Brown
About one mile S.W., this pioneer from S. C. settled on Nolichucky River in 1771. Brown's purchase of 2 tracts of land from the Cherokee on March 25, 1775, was made beneath a great oak tree still standing nearby. His sandstone marker reads "Jacob Brown, d. Jan. 25, 1785." The brick house nearby was built by his grandson, Byrd Brown, about 1800.

DAY TWO
(Tenn. 107) *Washington County, 13 miles south of Jonesboro*
1 A 91—Clarksville Iron Furnace
1.7 miles south are the ruins of the Clarksville Iron Furnace. The stone stack was built in 1833 by Montgomery Stuart, Elijah Embree and Edward West. The ore used was hauled in wagons across the mountain from the mines in Bumpass Cove. The iron produced was used locally and also was flatboated down the river as far as Alabama. Operations ceased in 1844.

(Tenn. 91) *Carter County, west of Bemberg Clubhouse*
1 A 16—Sycamore Shoals of the Watauga
In this neighborhood, on Sept. 26, 1780, Rev. Samuel Doak conducted religious services for the frontiersmen from Virginia and North Carolina, including the Watauga and other settlements in what is now Tennessee, upon the start of their campaign which resulted in the decisive victory of King's Mountain, on Oct. 7, 1780.

(Tenn. 91) *Carter County, .9 mile west of city limits of Elizabethton*
1 A 53—Watauga Purchase
Here, March 19, 1775, at the Sycamore Shoals, the Watauga Association, Charles Robertson, Trustee, bought from the Cherokee, with Oconostota as chief, lands along the Watauga, Holston and Great Canaway (now New) Rivers. The consideration for the purchase was 2000 Pounds Sterling.

(Tenn. 91) *Carter County, 1 mile west of city limits of Elizabethton*
1 A 52—Transylvania Purchase
In this valley, March 17, 1775, the Transylvania Company, led by Richard Henderson, John Williams, Thomas and Nathaniel Hart, bought from the Cherokee, led by Chief Oconostota, all lands between the Kentucky and Cumberland Rivers. Over 20 million acres sold for 2000 Pounds Sterling and goods worth 8000 Pounds.

(Tenn. 91) *Carter County, 1 mile west of city limits of Elizabethton*
1 A 8—Watauga Fort
400 yards northward and ½ mile northeast of the mouth of Gap Creek, stood Watauga Fort. Here, July 21, 1776, the settlers under Captain James Robertson repulsed the Cherokees under Old Abraham of Chilhowee, and Lt. John Sevier rescued "Bonny Kate" Sherrill.

(Tenn. 91) *Carter County, in Elizabethton, .75 mile east of Courthouse*
1 A 19—"The Mansion"
Built, 1780, by John Carter, Chairman of the Watauga Association, 1772, and his son, Landon. Carter County is named for the latter; Elizabethton is named for his wife, Elizabeth Maclin. The family cemetery is to the east of the house.

(U S 11 E) *Sullivan county, 5 miles south of Bluff City*
1 A 7—Rocky Mount
300 yards to the southeast is the restored home of William Cobb, pioneer. First seat of government of the Southwest Territory, October 10, 1790: Governor William Blount had headquarters here till removal to Knoxville, the new Capital, in 1792. Andrew Jackson lived here six weeks while waiting for a license to practice law.

Appendix I
John Sevier and William Blount

John Sevier   **William Blount**

John Sevier was called the handsomest man in Tennessee, and William Blount the next handsomest.

Appendix J
Pre-Tennessee Books
Published by The Overmountain Press

History of the Lost State of Franklin by Samuel Cole Williams, $21.95
(In-depth reference for use with this tour guide)

America's First Western Frontier by Brenda C. Calloway, $17.95
Antebellum Tennessee by Eric R. Lacy, $10.95
Beloved Mother: The Story of Nancy Ward by Charlotte Jane Ellington, $14.95
Dropped Stitches in Tennessee History by John Allison, $17.95
Jonesborough by Paul M. Fink, $14.95
The Melungeons by Bonnie Ball, $8.95
Nancy Ward / Dragging Canoe by Pat Alderman, $7.95
One Heroic Hour at King's Mountain by Pat Alderman, $7.95
The Overmountain Men by Pat Alderman, hardcover $22.95, softcover $17.95
Torchlights to the Cherokees by Robert Sparks Walker, $19.95
The Wataugans by Max Dixon, $6.95

The Overmountain Press
P.O. Box 1261
Johnson City, TN 37605
Call: 615-926-2691 • Fax: 615-929-2464

If not available from your local bookstore, orders may be sent to the above
address. Please include $2.00 shipping for first book, plus $1.00 for each
additional book. Tennessee residents must add 8½% sales tax.